Prayer
&
Confession

Look for these topics in the
Everyday Matters Bible Studies for Women

Acceptance	Mentoring
Bible Study & Meditation	Outreach
Celebration	Prayer
Community	Reconciliation
Confession	Sabbath & Rest
Contemplation	Service
Faith	Silence
Fasting	Simplicity
Forgiveness	Solitude
Gratitude	Stewardship
Hospitality	Submission
Justice	Worship

Prayer
&
Confession

Spiritual Practices
FOR EVERYDAY LIFE

Everyday Matters Bible Studies for Women—
Prayer & Confession

© 2014 Hendrickson Publishers Marketing, LLC
P. O. Box 3473
Peabody, Massachusetts 01961-3473

ISBN 978-1-61970-440-4

Printed in the United States of America

Contents

Confession

Holy Habits

Spiritual Practices for Everyday Life

Everyday life today is busier and more distracting than it has ever been before. While cell phones and texting make it easier to keep track of children and each other, they also make it harder to get away from the demands that overwhelm us. Time, it seems, is a shrinking commodity. But God, the Creator of time, has given us the keys to leading a life that may be challenging but not overwhelming. In fact, he offers us tools to do what seems impossible and come away refreshed and renewed. These tools are called spiritual practices, or spiritual disciplines.

Spiritual practices are holy habits. They are rooted in God's word, and they go back to creation itself. God has hardwired us to thrive when we obey him, even when it seems like his instructions defy our "common sense." When we engage in the holy habits that God has ordained, time takes on a new dimension. What seems impossible is actually easy; it's easy because we are tapping into God's resources.

The holy habits that we call spiritual practices are all geared to position us in a place where we can allow the Holy Spirit to work in us and through us, to grant us power and strength to do the things we can't do on our own. They take us to a place where we can become intimate with God.

While holy habits and everyday life may sound like opposites, they really aren't.

As you learn to incorporate spiritual practices into your life, you'll find that everyday life is easier. At the same time, you will draw closer to God and come to a place where you can luxuriate in his rich blessings. Here is a simple example. Elizabeth Collings hated running household errands. Picking up dry cleaning, doing the grocery shopping, and chauffeuring her kids felt like a never-ending litany of menial chores. One day she had a simple realization that changed her life. That day she began to use her "chore time" as a time of prayer and fellowship with God.

Whenever Elizabeth walked the aisle of the supermarket, she prayed for each person who would eat the item of food she selected. On her way to pick up her children, she would lay their lives out before God, asking him to be there for them even when she couldn't. Each errand became an opportunity for fellowship with God. The chore that had been so tedious became a precious part of her routine that she cherished.

The purpose of these study guides is to help you use spiritual practices to make your own life richer, fuller, and deeper. The series includes twenty-four spiritual practices that are the building blocks of Christian spiritual formation. Each practice is a holy habit that has been modeled for us in the Bible. The practices are acceptance, Bible study and meditation, celebration, community, confession, contemplation, faith, fasting, forgiveness, gratitude, hospitality, justice, mentoring, outreach, prayer, reconciliation, Sabbath and rest, service, silence, simplicity, solitude, stewardship, submission, and worship.

As you move through the practices that you select, remember Christ's promise in Matthew 11:28–30:

> *Come to me, all of you who are weary and carry heavy burdens. Take my yoke upon you. Let me teach you, because I am humble and gentle at heart, and you will find rest for your souls. For my yoke is easy to bear, and the burden I give you is light.*

Introduction

to the Practice of Prayer & Confession

In my heart and my soul
Lord, I give You control
Consume me from the inside out
Lord, let justice and praise
Become my embrace
To love You from the inside out.

—Hillsong United,
"From the Inside Out"

Our spiritual practices help us ask the questions at the heart of our lives. How do we live in God's presence, and how do we make his presence known? In prayer we abide in God's grace. We take up residence in God's presence as God comes to us.

Where do we begin? We begin on the ground, with our hearts prostrate in repentance, in adoration, in praise. The practices of prayer and confession lead to this holy space, this fertile ground. The rough ground is broken up to reveal rich soil. From this place of humility, so much can grow.

Our attitudes and actions help us answer the important questions. How will we embody the gospel? Our body, mind, soul—every part of us—are involved. They are intertwined so that there is less distance between thought and action, between the impetus to pray with or for someone and actually doing it. When someone takes time to pray with us and for us, that kind of love shocks us. But we seek to make it more common in our daily lives, to be the ones reaching out. Prayer is about being available—available to the Spirit, available to his love. Confession makes us available to the gaze of grace and mercy. We fear the prying eyes of those who want to bring us down. But God longs to raise us up. It begins with a posture of the heart and then works itself outward.

Prayer and confession are root disciplines. They focus on the core of what is essential to the Christ follower, our connection with God in Christ. They speak to what is at the center of our lives making our faith come alive. What does it mean for our faith to be living and active? God moves in us and moves us from the inside out. Our concerns shift from our own pain to the cry of the world. We feel the movement of the Spirit.

Sometimes the hardest part is showing up. Prayer and confession are about showing up and about what God shows us when we do: his unlimited love. By faith we have been brought to the banquet. In the end, time spent with God is not wasted. Time to sit at Jesus' feet, to reflect, to meditate, to strip away all our excuses, obstacles, and distractions. Our practice brings us here, into the presence of God, all for his glory. We are made right to bring his light to the world. God has bigger plans than just our own peace. He wants it for the whole world. Practicing prayer and confession gives us the chance to be peacemakers, to be a place where his glory dwells. We are changed not just to sit on our couches satisfied and sanctified, but in order to bring change and be change in the world. From this spiritual discipline, others can take root and flourish. From this practice, other practices emerge. These are at the core of our calling.

Where Love shows up, we want to follow. Prayer and confession help us to see God at work. The disciplines transform our whole selves—body, soul, heart, and mind. The movement of grace works in each area of our lives. Our bodies find postures of surrender and praise. Our souls are stilled to hear amid the swirling business of our lives, the voice of God calling us. Our hearts softened through humility and empathy as God draws us closer to his heart. Our minds sharpened and alert to seize every day.

These disciplines are at the fulcrum of our faith. The example of Christ guides us, and we look to examples around us and those who have come before. The grandmother who began and ended her day with prayer and wrote poems to express her faith. The coworker whose empathy is alive in everything she does. The stranger whose act of compassion wakes us from our apathy. The prayers of saints. The songs of struggle and victory. We seek to surround ourselves with a faith community who will encourage us, who will share our ups and downs and celebrate with us. We steep ourselves in healing waters of Scripture, which draws us to a deeper place.

We need to slough off the dead skin of sin, the callouses that no one wants to look at, those unfeeling places in us. How did we get here? How far away from you have we gone? The psalmist dredges the deep places, but we want to skim the surface. We want everything to be okay. We want to forget, but it's too tough for us to forgive the wounds caused by others. In confession, God brings us to a place where we can see our own faults and forgive others. We see how much God has done for us and we find joy. We live in newness of life (2 Corinthians 5:17).

Our disciplines help us acknowledge that our time here is short. What matters is the eternal in the everyday. What remains and what gives life to each day: the people whom prayer and confession allow us to see and serve with compassion, and the love that prayer and confession prompts to flow through us. Our spiritual practices help us make the most of our lives and bring meaning to each word and act. To bring God's care and concern for us into every aspect including what we put into our bodies, how we nourish our minds, and what occupies our time and actions. Every day, God works in us from the inside to bring wholeness and life so that our lives can shine as we share his grace.

Prayer

CHAPTER 1

Open Dialogue

Everyday Encounters with God

Lord, where do I put my hope?
My only hope is in you.

PSALM 39:7

For this study, read Psalm 39 and Matthew 6:5–15.

Before Skype and bad cell phone connections, and before the Fall knocked humanity off the cliff of sin, our natural state was seamless communication with God. But now we can breeze or trudge through a typical busy day, and by the time our heads hit the pillow we have answered e-mails, sent texts, made phone calls and posted status updates—the likelihood that a prayer crossed our lips might be even with the probability that we licked a stamp. There is static, a poor connection. Sometimes we can barely hear our own voice, let alone God's.

Through faith, God opened the way for us back to him. Through prayer, we open our hearts and minds to receive him and open our mouths to respond. Through the discipline of daily prayer, we have a chance to strengthen the connection God has established through faith. God reaches through the distance of distractions to open us to concerns beyond ourselves—in prayer we are connected to all believers. Our prayers show us candid snapshots of our relationship with God. One of the first glimpses we get of Jesus in his ministry is of him praying at his baptism. "As he was praying, the heavens were opened" (Luke 3:21). A dramatic conversation. But in the day-to-day, our prayers take on the mundane and profound.

The Psalms give us a wonderful and at times wonderfully messy view of authentic struggle and emotional whiplash, the raw and potent poetry of prayer. And here is where we see God's heart and his hope that our whole selves would join in. In Psalm 39, we find David in the midst of a passionate conversation. "A fire of words" is ignited within him and he asks God, "Remind me how brief my time on earth will be." He is at a place of struggle and questions, seeking perspective when emotions warp reality. "Hear my prayer, O Lord! Listen to my cries for help! Don't ignore my tears. For I am your guest—a traveler passing through" (Psalm 39:12). In this rough and real place, we get a glimpse of relationship—the open dialogue that God has invited us through faith to join, the eternal and everyday concerns intertwined and spoken in simple words, heart-rending emotion: "Help," "Listen," "Rescue Me."

David reminds us that in this brief life honesty matters more to God than spectacle. Our prayers don't always have to be pretty or eloquent. With each echo of his grace, with each new ray of sunlight, he invites us to call on him. He invites us just as we are to learn and love and listen to his voice and allow our heart to respond. We are in conversation, a constant communion, a daily dialogue. Our first groans and desires may take rough shape. We don't always know what to say or how to say it. What do we do with this breath, this fleeting life, this "fire of words"?

The Psalms give us a glimpse of a dynamic dialogue. David isn't afraid to come as he is, to bring God everything, even to share his fears and anger. The *Everyday Matters Bible for Women* explains that "Psalms does not follow one continuous narrative. Instead, its poems and prayers capture many different moments in a believer's relationship with God."

In unexpected moments—a gasp, a cry, a lump in the throat—prayer brings awareness of the divine. As simple as a prayer of thanks as sunlight warms our face on a brisk winter walk, or when we find a parking spot, or as complicated as putting thoughts and words together after hearing the diagnosis. From the slightest paper cut to the largest life-altering decision, cultivating the habit of prayer transforms our everyday moments as God guides the conversation. There is no space in our lives that God does not want to occupy with his presence. Whether our hands folded and head bowed. Whether we are singing with a praise song on the radio. Whether in whispers or in wails. God wants it all. Sometimes our prayers are in the form of a question, sometimes a lit candle, sometimes the long exhale as a light goes out. God meets us where we are.

Robert J. Morgan in the *Everyday Matters Bible for Women* talks about the powerful example of Ruth Bell Graham who prayed the Scriptures by inserting her name and claiming God's promises, "speaking them back to God." Our lives become the text. The words of Scripture lift off the pages and onto our tongues. We grab the words out of the air from songs and car horns. We piece together a meditation. Each new experience, each new day is the prayer of our lives where we find and set our course. Prayer is a place where our actions and attitude join to pursue God's purpose for us.

God calls every part of us to enter into a lifelong discourse. We take our cue from Christ, who lived a life in seamless conversation with the Father. Prayer helps us put life in perspective and focus on what is important. We are called to live the prayers we speak. When we pray for peace, God is calling us to live that peace. When we ask for forgiveness, God is calling us to forgive (Matthew 6:14–15).

Prayer is a discipline that feeds us from the inside out. The Spirit moves in our lives and helps us to look outside ourselves. Prayer nourishes us for the journey, and it makes the other disciplines possible. It helps to define us as belonging to Christ (1 Thessalonians 5:18).

When was the first time you prayed? When was the last time? Did the conversation stop? When did the words dry up? When did the words start bouncing against an invisible wall? When did the words get stuck in your throat? Was it doubt? Was it distraction? Was it apathy? Can you even identify the place where the excuses became a distant memory, a hollow echoing, a voice once thundering, once calming, now elusive? Does prayer seem irrelevant? We say the same words and they evaporate. When did we start feeling defeated by this discipline before we even started? God opens our hearts and starts the dialogue, one thought in front of the other, one word connected to another word, and pretty soon we're talking. Pretty soon the conversation is flowing. But first, we have to open our mouths.

Prayer is not an escape, but rather a way of entering God's presence. All aspects of our lives are invited to join in. There isn't a part of us that is off limits. We open up and God draws us to go deeper. In the stillness and in the chaos, we find God at the center. "My entire lifetime is just a moment to you; at best, each of us is but a breath" (Psalm 39:5). Here in the swirl of concerns, God comes to us. We do not have to wait for just the right moment to bow our hearts. The prayer has already begun.

"I have learned that prayer is not asking for what you think you want but asking to be changed in ways you can't imagine." —Kathleen Norris, Amazing Grace

As you study this chapter, create a timeline of your faith journey.

1. Think about how prayer has been a part of your life. What have been some memorable prayer moments? Why were they special?

2. What does your daily prayer life look like? What are some of the things that help you to pray and what are some of your struggles?

3. Read Matthew 6:5–15. How does this prayer reflect the attitudes and actions God wants us to have when we pray?

4. Throughout the Psalms, David and others make prayer seem so natural and effortless. It is as if God is right there. But a common complaint is that God feels distant. What have we replaced prayer with in our daily lives? What other things do we use instead of bringing everything to God?

5. How is God drawing you deeper through prayer? What have you learned thus far about prayer? What are some ways you can share your journey with others?

6. Whether it's using an app on your phone or a sticky note, create reminders to pray. How can we repurpose things we already own to help call our attention to prayer?

Points to Ponder

In Philippians 4:6, Paul says to "pray about everything. Tell God what you need, and thank him for all he has done." We might spend a lot of time thinking about something or worrying about it, but praying about it might not be in the picture.

- What seems too insignificant for prayer? Why? How does God use even what seems insignificant to bring us closer to him?

Paul also tells followers of Christ to "devote yourselves to prayer with an alert mind and a thankful heart" (Colossians 4:2).

- How are devotion, alertness, and thankfulness important aspects of a life of prayer?

"May your prayer and your living be so closely connected that you cannot separate your day plan from your Amen." —Emily P. Freeman

Prayer

Lord, you are closer than the words we speak. Closer than the air we breathe. You draw us deeper into you, into a life of love and abundant joy. Thank you for beginning the eternal dialogue through faith. Help us to weave the fragments of grace that surround us throughout our day into a life of prayer. All for your glory. All to make you known.

Add your prayer in your own words.

Amen.

Put It into Practice

This week, unpack your prayers. What are the prayers you have carried with you? What are the prayers you say every day? Take the opportunity to write them down. As we grow more intentional in prayer, we look at where we are, where we have been, and where by the grace of God we are going.

Take-away Treasure

God invites us daily to join in the ongoing conversation of faith. Sometimes we don't have any words. Sometimes we have too many. God fills in the gaps with his grace, making up for what we lack. Each day we both begin again and join in the lifelong exchange, bringing all that we are before the Lord to use. Whether in exaltation or exasperation, we come as we are and are met with love that doesn't leave us the same.

CHAPTER 2

A Heart That Hears You

The Lesson of Listening

"Let my words fall like rain on tender grass,
like gentle showers on young plants."

DEUTERONOMY 32:2

For this study, read 1 Samuel 1 and 3:1–14 and Psalm 5.

I feel for Hannah. Things didn't go as planned. The life she had dreamed of was still just a dream, and the one she was living was a nightmare. The baby she desperately wanted didn't come. Instead, bitterness was born out of jealousy and anguish. And here in this place of frustration and pain, she poured it all out. The incomprehensible mess of it. In a reckless prayer that looked like drunken gibberish, she bared it all before God. Sometimes waiting is the hardest prayer of all.

But just when it all looked so hopeless, God met the cry of Hannah's heart. Her response was immediate—a prayer of praise and an act of sacrifice and surrender, her son given over to God's service, acknowledging that the gift was not hers but God's. So "Samuel grew up in the presence of the Lord" (1 Samuel 2:21). Hannah reminds us that the answers to our prayers do not belong to us.

This child born out of prayer grows in faith and hears a voice calling. Guided by Eli, he responds with the words our lives must echo: "Speak, Lord, your servant is listening" (1 Samuel 3:9). Samuel's response is immediate, a life of faithful service, the ears of those who had turned their deaf hearts away from God. Samuel continues to hear from God and to communicate messages to the people. He continues to advise them to listen to God's voice (1 Samuel 12:14), even though the words and warnings go ignored.

The stories of Hannah's and Samuel's lives are not tidy. It's like our lives. Often in the midst of the mess is where we meet God. When we listen in prayer, we acknowledge that we are not our own. God has bigger plans. In prayer we enter in, abiding in God's presence. Whether our eyes are opened or closed, in that place where our voice and vision are surrendered in silence, there is space for a greater view to emerge. When we listen through meditating on Scripture, we are joined with the saints from every time and place before the throne. We are reminded of eternity. Even Jesus surrendered in prayer and listened to the Father: "Yet I want your will to be done, not mine" (Luke 22:42). God had bigger plans.

Listening in prayer is a form of seeking God. Listening is letting go of our control to the One who grasps the future with calm assurance. We are not always sure where the conversation will lead. At the end of our lives, is the point of it all to say that life turned out exactly as we planned and expected? No, God's vision embraces so much more than we can see. His hope is much broader, and his love is much deeper. When we listen to God, we give ourselves over to that deeper life and to accomplishing "infinitely more than we might ask or think" (Ephesians 3:20). When we listen in prayer, we trust. God helps us grow our prayers from thimble-sized wishes to oceans of grace. We ask for a fish and when he calls us to cast our nets on the other side, they begin to burst. By listening, we learn what to ask for.

When we begin our day with the simple prayer—"Help me to listen"—our focus shifts from ourselves to the One who gives strength and courage to face the day, whatever it brings. When we listen in prayer, our attention is tuned and our thoughts turn to others. Listening is a chance to hear God's heartbeat for the world. God-listener Meister Eckhart says, "The best and most wonderful thing that can happen to you in this life is that you should be silent and let God work and speak."

Prayer puts us at the feet of Jesus. We are there with Mary while Martha paces distracted in the background. We are there in the crowds. We are there with the multitude before the throne. We are there to learn. Prayer puts our hearts in surrender. Prayer makes us available to the call we might otherwise ignore. When we listen in prayer, it puts our feet on the right path. Our feet follow Jesus as we love and serve. "Tune your ears to wisdom, and concentrate on understanding. Cry out for insight, and ask for understanding. Search for them as you would for silver; seek them like hidden treasures" (Proverbs 2:2–4).

As we listen in prayer, we see how God is speaking to us—all around us. We let a beautiful piece of music or a crying child awaken us to hear God in a new way. We wrestle our hearts away from distractions. We let our prayers begin with "Amen," an acknowledgement that before any other words leave our lips, we know that the gift of this life is not our own.

Let your will be done, Lord. Let us cultivate hearts that hear you. Let our lives be more receptive to your presence. To not only listening but acting on the words of life you give. Let our response be immediate—faithfulness, service, surrender.

"Listen to your life. See it for the fathomless mystery it is. In the boredom and pain of it, no less than in the excitement and gladness: touch, taste, smell your way to the holy and hidden heart of it, because in the last analysis all moments are key moments, and life itself is grace." —Frederick Buechner

"There is not in the world a kind of life more sweet and delightful than that of a continual conversation with God."
—Brother Lawrence, The Practice of the Presence of God

As you study this chapter, reflect on ways of listening to God.

1. There are so many excuses people used in the Bible for not listening to God. What distracts you most from listening in prayer? How can you use what distracts you not as an excuse but as a point of entry?

2. Jesus often went out to find quiet moments to pray alone. Stillness is so hard to come by. What are some ways that you can find quiet even in your hectic life (car rides alone, walks, early morning or late at night)?

3. Some heard an audible voice. Others saw God's presence in remarkable ways and were called to attention. When we don't have a burning bush or words written on a wall, however, how do we know that what we hear is from God? What are some ways we can seek wisdom and discernment?

4. Are there answers to prayer that we have not acted on or acknowledged because they were different from what we wanted or expected? Jonah is an example of someone who heard and went the other way. How do we incorporate acting on the outcomes of our listening?

5. How can we listen as a community? How can God speak through others?

6. How do we "listen" with our senses? Listening through music, art, word, poetry, photography, observing the world around us—from nature to the news—how can we hear the words of God in our surroundings?

Points to Ponder

"His purpose was for the nations to seek after God and perhaps feel their way toward him and find him—though he is not far from any one of us. For in him we live and move and exist" (Acts 17:27–28).

- How does prayer help us to understand more about the attributes of God?

"For God speaks again and again, though people do not recognize it" (Job 33:14). God speaks words of warning and discipline.

- Is the problem that we do not *hear* God or that we do not *like* what we hear? How do we respond to tough words?

"To say that 'prayer changes things' is not as close to the truth as saying, 'Prayer changes me and then I change things.'" —Oswald Chambers, My Utmost for His Highest

Prayer

God, so often I come with my lists. I come with my agenda. I come ready to tell you how the world and my life should be. I come with demands and complaints instead of just sitting at your feet *to listen*. God, open my ears to hear you. Open my mind to understand. Open my heart to receive. Your words are life. Your wisdom is truth.

Add your prayer in your own words.

Amen.

Put It into Practice

This week, think about the ratio of speaking to listening that you do. What have you been missing that those around you have been saying? What are the repeated messages you haven't taken in or taken time to act on? Make an effort to listen more. How is God using those around you to help you form your prayers?

Take-away Treasure

God wants to give us words of life, but often we get in the way. When we clear a path for the Spirit, God shows up in remarkable ways. Listening takes our attention off ourselves and focuses it on God, the source and support we seek.

CHAPTER 3

Keeping On

The Persistent Path of Prayer

Rejoice in our confident hope. Be patient
in trouble, and keep on praying.

ROMANS 12:12

For this study, read Romans 12, Psalm 86, and Luke 18:1–8.

It would be one thing if God just wanted us to pray. Add it
to the "to do" list and get it over with. But God encourages
us to keep on praying, even at times for the same thing—
the thing that seems to provoke only silence from God. We
pray in whispers and we pray in roars. We put the prayer on
repeat. But the diagnosis remains the same. The cold shoul-
der doesn't soften. So what has changed? At times we're not
even sure if we hear our own voice, let alone God's. "The
blessing of persistence in prayer," Patricia Raybon says in the
Everyday Matters Bible for Women, "is that it brings us, over
and over, into the presence of God. We form a pattern of
coming to him." Not just once, but over and over again.

Prayer brings us back, not to the problem but into the presence of the one who cares beyond our understanding. We are brought back to the beauty of humility. Brought back to waiting, to listening and seeking, reminded that God finds the way through the wilderness.

Three times a day, Daniel prayed. Three times a day, he drew into the presence of God, the Creator and Sustainer of the universe. Three times a day, Daniel showed up. He prayed. It didn't matter what the weather was like or what mood he was in or whether someone was going to kill him if he did. And when the very real threats were made, he remained praying: "[He] knelt down as usual in his upstairs room . . . just as he had always done, giving thanks to his God" (Daniel 6:10). And when the very real accusers came knocking at his door, there he was "praying and asking for God's help" (Daniel 6:11). And when they tried to kill him, the very real God remained, present and powerful.

Our persistent prayers also speak to God's presence and power in our lives, even if our experiences aren't as dramatic. Daniel's example in the face of danger puts our excuses in perspective. It looked like it was the end, but Daniel's persistent obedience even in the face of danger brought a new beginning not just for himself, but for the whole land after he emerged from the mouths of the lions unscathed.

Daniel's story speaks to the truth that might sometimes be hard to see. We might not always feel the presence and power. It might feel like our faith is at the end, ready to give it all up if we don't get the response we long for. But God wants us to enter into a life of prayerful obedience and realize what action in the face of obstacles can do. Persistence in prayer keeps us going in the right direction, keeps us focused and following. The dangers we face are more insidious. Sometimes the only obstacles we have to overcome are laziness, apathy, and busyness. But these can be just as deadly, and we don't realize what they are doing to us. Daniel's discipline, by surrendering to the only One who had real authority, gave him the power to face difficulties with thanks, and to come again and again into God's presence.

When we are persistent in our prayers, the relationship still might not work out, the sick friend might die, the coworker might not forgive, the check might bounce anyway. We have obstacles and circumstances that threaten to discourage us and distance us from God, but "despite all these things, overwhelming victory is ours through Christ, who loved us" (Romans 8:37). Persistence in prayer keeps us in the victory we have in Christ despite our circumstances. When it seems that all that surrounds us is unspeakable misery, God's work in and through us continues. Our circumstances can stun and stunt us. They can leave us dejected and depressed. But instead of turning in on ourselves or turning away from God, that is a time to "pray and never give up" (Luke 18:1).

Why is God so persistent about persistence? Why do we need to keep coming back to the door and knocking? God doesn't want us to lose heart. Ultimately, it is God's love that presses us to press on. The problems to which our repeated prayers attest are meant to build us up: "Endurance develops strength of character, and character strengthens our confident hope of salvation. And this hope will not lead to disappointment. For we know how dearly God loves us, because he has given us the Holy Spirit to fill our hearts with his love" (Romans 5:4–5).

What is the refrain of our lives? Unfortunately, complaining is often the one constant and our annoyances only get amplified. But God wants us to connect with the deeper concerns every day and *everywhere*. I've prayed in stadiums, Gothic cathedrals, kneeling in my grandparents' home, in hospitals, or in huts. It doesn't matter if we're standing at the kitchen sink or in the boardroom. God remains the same. It is we who are changed. A life of continuous prayer turns car rides into holy space and "at the end of my rope" into a place where hope breaks through.

When we live in ceaseless prayer, we live in the eternal. We cannot be shaken. We return to the source of our strength. Over and over, our vulnerabilities become strengths. Again and again, God brings us his unending love. Even when easy answers evade us, we know that God's faithfulness wins. We press on. We don't give up. We turn from our own concerns to focus the gaze of grace on those around us.

"And every step every breath you are there
Every tear every cry every prayer
In my hurt at my worst
When my world falls down
Not for a moment will You forsake me."
—Meredith Andrews, *"Not for a Moment"*

*As you study this chapter, think about
what is ceaseless in your life.*

1. We often seek a formula for prayer. How is praying without ceasing different from just praying more or in a certain way?

2. In Psalm 86, David presents his requests, and it's a pretty big list: "I am calling on you constantly" (86:3). Why does God want to take on himself our complaints, problems, and pain?

3. With all the pressures of life, we sometimes seek an escape. What does entering God's presence through prayer cause us to leave behind? How does prayer cause us instead to embrace and engage the world?

4. The examples of prayer postures in Scripture are varied from prostrated to hands lifted high and everything in between. What is the posture of prayer most common or comfortable to you? How does your physical posture affect your prayers?

5. In James 5:13–18, it says that a prayer offered in faith will heal. So if a prayer for healing doesn't work, does that mean the person didn't have faith or enough faith?

6. In her *Everyday Matters Bible for Women* reflection, Cindy Crosby talks about the ways she has incorporated "journaling, walking, and drawing" into her prayer practice. What are some other activities that enrich your prayers?

Points to Ponder

In *Jewish Prayer: The Origins of Christian Liturgy,* Carmine DiSante says that "prayer, like life itself, is in one way always the same and in another always new." Sometimes sameness seems like something stable and reliable and sometimes it can seem boring.

- What attitudes have you attached to repeated prayer? What has been your experience with repetition in prayer? How can you refresh your view of prayer?

The Way of a Pilgrim explores an unknown Russian peasant's attempts to "pray without ceasing," but he finds that "laziness, boredom, drowsiness and a cloud of disturbing thoughts" kept him from prayer.

- What keeps you from prayer?

*"Keep on asking. . . . Keep on seeking. . . .
Keep on knocking." (Luke 11:9)*

Prayer

God, by your grace and mercy, you encompass my fear and doubt. Your love is all consuming. You seek to replace what was once void with the praise and prayers of your people. Help my voice of thanks to be unending. Turn my chronic complaints into ceaseless prayer. Thank you for transforming me by your Spirit. Help me to live in you.

Add prayer in your own words.

Amen.

Put It into Practice

This week, filter everything through prayer, asking, "What would happen if I prayed about this?" Then make prayer a first, instead of a last, resort. Look for ways to put prayer first in your life.

Take-away Treasure

At the end of the day we never say, "Oh, I wish I hadn't prayed about that!" We don't regret bringing things to God. And God encourages us to live seamlessly in his presence and at work in the world, not letting the sacred be relegated to a reserved space or be made irrelevant. Bringing everything before God to be transformed and redeemed.

CHAPTER 4

Lifting Up

Praying Together and for Others

They held gold bowls filled with incense,
which are the prayers of God's people.
And they sang a new song.

REVELATION 5:8-9

For this study, read Luke 5:17–26 and Psalm 141.

"Can I pray for you?" It's not a question we get asked very often. And looking back, we ask ourselves, "Have I ever asked that question?" Maybe an even better question is, "How can I pray for you?" Our life of prayer takes us into each other's lives as well, and through prayer we are linked. We learn what it is to live in community as the body of Christ. We are taken out of ourselves, and our limited view, and see the world with another's eyes. We grow in empathy as God grows our heart for others.

The worship service had ended, and the room was hot and humid as the group of college students I was traveling with in India began to hear the stories of the women gathered there. Through a translator, they poured out their stories of heartache and struggle (many of them were living with HIV). "How can I pray for you?" The simple question took on new significance—for families torn apart due to their outcast status, for constant pain, for work so they could support themselves, even for the will to live. We prayed with these women, and as the room slowly began to clear, one student was still praying. Kneeling on the floor at the feet of a woman, she touched her and poured out her heart on behalf of this sister—lifting her up through prayer.

When I read Revelation 5:8–9, I think about her prayer. I think about the prayers we pray every day—the prayers of God's people. What a thought that our prayers are not lost, that they blend together before the Lord and create a rich incense, a pleasing aroma. Prayer connects us with God and each other and believers of every time and place. Our struggles and joys are not our own. Even in the midst of them, we can realize that we are joined with others in the Spirit—"Accept my prayer as incense offered to you, and my upraised hands as an evening offering" (Psalm 141:2)—together, forever praising God, the ultimate picture of that eternal gathering with all the saints.

Lifting up the paralyzed man onto the roof, they put their prayers into action. They brought a man to Jesus, the only one who could help and truly heal. Together their feet followed their faith. "Interceding for others is a way of loving them, deeply and meaningfully," Tracy Balzer shares in the *Everyday Matters Bible for Women.* If I want to show that I love you, I will pray for you. I will pray with you. I will lift you up.

Our prayers together bring life to us and to others. We realize through our prayers the power of what Love can do—when we pray together in worship and praise as our voices join together in harmony, when we pray with a child whose inquisitive faith is a light bulb of curious intensity and joy, when we pray with a seasoned saint whose love has endured heartbreak and hardships. Our prayers come together with the intervening voices of others to fill the space where doubt and despair would like to take up residence in our hearts.

What can happen when someone prays for you? Jesus prays for us and shows us what is at the heart of our relationship: compassion. Jesus' prayer shows us the power of what Love can do. We want prayer to be easy and pretty. But prayer takes us past piety to repentance: "Father, forgive them" (Luke 23:34). Jesus' words reveal who we are and who God is and how we are called to look outside our own concerns to others. God knows what we need most. And what the world around us longs for.

We are to be community. And when we come together in prayer, we sing a new song. God binds us to others and brings us out of ourselves, sharing the concerns of the world and opening us up to a daily dialogue of grace and mercy. Our faith is not for us only, but for everyone, and God draws us together to pray for one another and to pray for the world.

We need time alone in prayer, but we also need communal time—shared time. When we practice the discipline of prayer, integrating it seamlessly into every aspect of our daily lives, we are not the only ones who are changed. We are not the only ones who are lifted up. The light reaches further. Joy spreads. A fire of faith is reignited through the Holy Spirit. Our prayers remain, together with other believers from all times and places, a pleasing aroma, an offering of praise.

"Kindle in our hearts, O God, the flame of that love which never ceases, that it may burn in us, giving light to others. May we shine forever in your temple, set on fire with your eternal light, even your Son Jesus Christ, our Saviour and our Redeemer. Amen." —*The Prayer of St. Columba*

"Pray in the Spirit at all times and on every occasion. Stay alert and be persistent in your prayers for all believers everywhere." (Ephesians 6:18)

As you study this chapter, consider how you can partner with others in prayer.

1. God gives us encouragement and tells us that he is with us as we gather in his name: "For where two or three gather together as my followers, I am there among them" (Matthew 18:20). How can you make gathering for prayer with others and for others a daily priority? What are some of the obstacles you have encountered? How can you overcome these?

2. In 2 Kings 20:1–10 Hezekiah asks for a miracle, something only God could do. When he was sick and found out he was going to die, he asked to have more time. Then he asked for a sign, a turning back of the sundial. God sent his promise, saying to him through Isaiah: "I will rescue you and this city . . . for my own honor." Are we bold with God? Do we ask for things that only God can do? How do we sometimes get stuck in small-mindedness? We don't know how much time we have left. What will we do with the time we have been given?

3. What are some of the ways Jesus prayed with and for others?

4. Who are the people around you whom you can serve through prayer? What are the areas in your life where you need to humble yourself and ask for prayer? How can you join with others for prayer on a regular basis?

5. In her *Everyday Matters Bible for Women* reflection, Caryn Rivadeneira says that "almost nothing else can duplicate the bonds of a trusted community of believers who together lift their worries and brokenness to our merciful, redeeming God." How can we cultivate the bonds of trust in community?

6. What would it take to cultivate a prayer movement in your community? Start with the spark in your own heart and see what God ignites.

Points to Ponder

When our own worries get too big, we wonder why God would want us to take on the burden of others. "I urge you, first of all, to pray for all people. Ask God to help them; intercede on their behalf, and give thanks for them" (1 Timothy 2:1).

- How does praying for others put our concerns in perspective?

Read Luke 5:17–26. John writes: "Let's not merely say that we love each other; let us show the truth by our actions. Our actions will show that we belong to the truth" (1 John 3:18–19).

• How does the example in Luke reflect John's admonition? How can we intercede on behalf of others through our prayers put into action?

"Total involvement in prayer demands of us a participation in society, in the lives of those close to us, of those at a distance, of intimate friends, and of strangers." —Jacques Ellul

Prayer

God, you made us for community. Prayer is a gift that connects us to you and to each other. Thank you for strengthening your church throughout the world through the Spirit's work of prayer. Help us to get a glimpse of that eternal communion in every word we speak on another's behalf. Grow us into a grateful and graceful community of love drawing more people to you.

Add your prayer in your own words.

Amen.

Put It into Practice

This week, join with others in prayer. Whether you are across the dinner table or miles apart on Skype, pray with someone else and for someone else. Let another lift your worries to the Lord and feel the strength of the community of faith.

Take-away Treasure

God wants us to experience the blessing of prayer. He wants us to extend that blessing to the world and help others to find connection and community through Christ. You don't have to start with a stadium full of people—just one other believer who will join with you. Then watch as your faith and community grow.

Notes / Prayer Requests

Notes / Prayer Requests

_____

_____

_____

_____

_____

_____

_____

_____

_____

_____

_____

_____

_____

_____

_____

_____

Confession

CHAPTER 1

Opening Up

Everyday Encounters with Grace

"But let us fall into the hands of the
LORD, for his mercy is great."

2 SAMUEL 24:14

For this study, read Psalms 51 and 139 and 2 Samuel 12.

An annoying message pops up on my computer screen. "A connection failure has occurred," it blankly states. I blink back angrily at the screen and click the little red "x" in the corner of the box, fuming under my breath and hoping the problem goes away. I don't want to deal with it. Maybe it will magically disappear. But it keeps coming back. I have to get to the source if I want to find a solution instead of staying disconnected and not able to get anything done.

In our lives, it might be easier if a message popped up, a little bubble in the air that diagnosed our problems. It would still be annoying, but at least we would be reminded to do something about it. Our lives get cluttered up with sin. "A connection failure has occurred." We need to confess. We are not able to accomplish with joy our spiritual practices because unconfessed sin gets in the way. Confession is a root discipline. It can't be ignored.

In 2 Samuel 12, Nathan sends David a message about the ugly truth that his life has become. Through a vivid story, he hopes to convey what David has done that has caused such a catastrophic disconnect. But David has a hard time getting the memo. He doesn't want to see that the truth applies to him. God had blessed David with everything he could want, but still he wasn't satisfied. Through a series of choices, David followed the slippery slope of sin in one bad move after another. But God finally breaks through and brings clarity, and David confesses and comes clean. The discipline of confession brings us back to reality and to thankfulness. Our eyes are opened to all God has done for us and we can live in joy again. The connection is restored.

It's much easier to get excited about some of the other spiritual disciplines. We might wake up bursting with energy ready to worship or celebrate or serve. But when confession is on the day's agenda, we hit the snooze button. We would rather wait until our deathbed to confess than gladly submit to this discipline in our daily lives. Sure, we can find time to read the Bible or say a prayer. But confession often gets ignored. We might think that as we go along in our life of faith, we will confess less. Yet as we look at the great examples of faith, we see that as their hearts and lives were turned toward God and his purpose, confession flowed. The more we encounter God, the more we see our lives in contrast and ask for God's mercy, thanking him for what he has done.

We come from a long line of the confession averse. At the beginning of our salvation story, fingers point in every direction, excuses are made, blame and shame instead of awed humility when God asks Adam and Eve, "What have you done?" Every day, we live with the ramifications of a broken world, and the brokenness is not as far from us as we would like to think. We live *with* sin, but we don't have to live *in* it. We live in Christ, alive to the hope he has for us. We live with the frustrations and factions of a fractured world. God calls us not to cover up the faults and failings but to confess.

We have a choice. How will we spend our day? What will we think about? How will we respond to the calling of faith? When our house is a mess, we clean it. When the car breaks down, we get it fixed. But when we sin, it isn't always so easy. We try to ignore it. We do all kinds of things to avoid it. Some sins are so obvious, others so insidious. Part of us goes numb, we grow frustrated and distracted, we feel lost. But confession brings us back to the start. God helps us find our way again.

We need to ask ourselves what is getting in the way in our relationship with others and with God. When we are able to give honest answers and see how the truth applies to us, we are able to open up so that we can give—and when we are open, we can also receive. The alternative is a hardened heart, a turning inward, a turning away. We can keep clicking the red "x" but the problem remains.

When we confess, we can move beyond ourselves. In *A Prayer Journal*, Flannery O'Connor shares our common dilemma: "Dear God, I cannot love Thee the way I want to. You are the slim crescent of a moon that I see and my self is the earth's shadow that keeps me from seeing all the moon. . . . I do not know You God because I am in the way. Please help me to push myself aside." If we can just get out of the way, there is room for God to use us. Confession keeps us at a place of humility, open to what God has for us. We are connected. We stay in Christ. Confession helps us open up to others and to God.

This is one of those moments where we have to put on the oxygen mask first before we can help others—we need to deal with our own dirt first. Without confession, the other disciplines won't be rooted in real joy. We will be trying to earn brownie points instead of earnestly seeking the One who has done it all for us. When we don't confess our sins, we distance ourselves and the Spirit's call is dulled. With confession comes life. David sings out to God and generations to come follow Jesus as he crosses the slope to Calvary. "Create in me a clean heart, O God. Renew a loyal spirit within me. . . . Restore to me the joy of your salvation, and make me willing to obey you" (Psalm 51:10, 12).

"True guilt has a directional movement, first pointing backward to the sin and then pointing forward to repentance." —Philip Yancey, "The Gift of Guilt," Everyday Matters Bible for Women

1. William F. May speaks of sin as "whatever we do that violates our life in God." What is the definition of sin? If we are born into sin, why are we held responsible and called to confess our sins?

2. God wants to give us good gifts, but sometimes we block that through our disobedience. How does confession make way for God's grace?

3. What questions should we ask ourselves when we confess? What if we don't feel any different afterwards? How do we know we are forgiven?

4. Why does God take our sin so seriously if he forgives it anyway?

5. How often should we confess? If confession makes us more aware of sin in our lives, isn't that a bad thing?

6. What are the sins we struggle with the most? Why is pride such a struggle for us, and why is there such an admonition against it?

Points to Ponder

In 2 Samuel 24:24, David professes, "I will not present burnt offerings to the Lord my God that have cost me nothing."

- Why is there always a cost associated with sin? How is sacrifice part of confession?

- Read Psalm 139:23–24. How do we let God examine us? What are some of the sins hidden in plain sight?

"This is true repentance when the heart internally through sorrow and regret is broken down, destroyed, laid low, and by faith and forgiveness of sins is made holy, consoled, purified, changed, and made better so that an external improvement in life follows." —Johann Arndt, True Christianity

Prayer

God, you give me life and I thank you that—as Paul writes in Romans 5:6—"when we were utterly helpless, Christ came at just the right time and died for us sinners." My life is held in your grace, and by your mercy I am free. Let my heart break with whatever breaks your heart. Help me to bring everything before you. Lay my heart bare, and take all my days and make them yours.

Add your prayer in your own words.

Amen.

Put It into Practice

This week, think of all the areas of your life where you would like a clean slate. What has happened to bring you to this place? Write down the situations that need to be righted. Take an honest look at your role and how confession is the beginning of that process.

Take-away Treasure

We don't have to look too far to find the source of many problems and unhappiness. We would like to point the finger at someone, anyone else. But when we go beyond the surface, when our faith takes us deeper to deal with the real issues, we see how our sin causes the disconnect. From the places of deep pain, God longs to bring his healing love. The practice of confession opens us to receive and to give. We go from scrounging for crumbs to a feast—from scarcity to limitless, boundless, endless grace.

CHAPTER 2

Letting Go

From Failure to Unfailing Love

"Return to the LORD your God, for he is
merciful and compassionate, slow to get
angry and filled with unfailing love."

JOEL 2:13

For this study, read Psalms 38 and 103 and Joel 2:12–27

I did a lot of running around barefoot outdoors as a child,
though I knew I shouldn't and the sharp pain in my foot
reminded me why. I got a lot of splinters. And if I didn't go
right to my dad—the keeper of the tweezers—and admit it,
the splinter would go deeper, the pain would become un-
bearable, and I would hobble along. Just saying "I'm sorry, I
won't do it again" wouldn't fix it. Somebody's got to do some
digging. It might hurt, but it's the only way it's really going
to heal. Likewise, confession isn't just our words: God's love
is worked out in our lives in action and in truth.

If God loves us, does it really have to be this way? Do we
have to deal with the pain?

51

In Psalm 38, David goes into uncomfortable detail about how his sin has affected him physically, and it isn't pretty: "I am exhausted and completely crushed. My groans come from an anguished heart" (Psalm 38:8). The sorrow is deep, but God goes with us even deeper to root it out, to bring redemption.

Through confession, we are called to be truth-seekers—to go beneath the surface, to wrestle with the uncomfortable. Our change comes from within and affects everything. Confession touches every aspect of our lives, our relationships, and how we view the world. But it is worth it. It can get ugly at times, but through it all God draws us closer to himself.

Sin calls for something drastic. God took drastic measures for us, and he doesn't just want our words or our lip service—he wants it all. We have been using a Band-Aid when we need an ax or a shovel. We should not be making space for self-pity or false pride; we should be making room for the Spirit, for God's love to flood in. What we cover over, God wants to cleanse.

We have to find the source, and we go through the guilt to get there. When we first get into trouble as children, our first instructions are, "Say you're sorry!" But being sorry is more than words or a feeling. We can't let go of something we don't recognize, so therefore our confession begins with recognizing sin. Part of the discipline is taking time to examine our lives—making space every day to listen to God through prayer, meditation, Bible study, and reflection. We recognize and we release. We grieve. There isn't a shortcut or a quick fix. Martin Luther reminds us in his morning prayer that God wants our "body, soul and all things." There is a distance between us and God that we can't travel on our own. Christ journeys with us.

When we let go of failures, we also let go of the excuses that keep us from pursuing the excellence and joy God desires us to experience. Confession helps us to see ourselves and each other in right relationship. In Luke's Gospel we see a woman moved beyond words. The truth is known among those who gather and point fingers. They would rather recognize her sin than recognize her as a fellow human being in need of compassion. They do not want to release her sin; they would rather remind her and try to feel better about themselves. In remembering others' sins, we try to cover up our own. It is easier to bring up others' faults than to confess. The woman comes with the truth, with beautiful perfume poured on Jesus' feet. In recognizing the truth of who she is, she also reveals the truth of who Jesus is: the way, the truth, and the life. She brings attention to him instead of to herself. And her brave act of faith leaves the Pharisees focused on Jesus, asking, "Who is this man?" This One who brings forgiveness.

Our confession brings us back to life, back to living in the truth of God's grace and love. Through the beauty of her actions, through her tears and selflessness, her confession was heard. God wants more than words from us as well. He wants us to follow with our body and soul: "Give me your hearts. Come. . . ." (Joel 2:12). Here, in confession, our hearts are poured out. In that place where there are no words, where we have hit the end of our understanding, we fall at his feet. And God does not leave us empty and abandoned. This is the place where God's words lift us: "Your sins are forgiven." We are left with his peace, a hope, and a future.

"I truly live only whenever I am conscious of him [God] and seek him. 'What, then, do I seek?' a voice cried out within me. 'He is there, the one without whom there could be no life.' To know God and to live come to one and the same thing. God is life." —Leo Tolstoy, Confessions

As you study this chapter, reflect on what keeps you from living fully in Christ.

1. In Psalm 38:4, David cries out, "My guilt overwhelms me—it is a burden too heavy to bear." What are some ways God uses to help us recognize our sin? How do we recognize the effects of sin?

2. What is our response to sin and what is God's? List some attributes of God that speak to his forgiveness.

3. In Joel 2:12, God says, "Turn to me now, while there is time." There is urgency, so why do we always want to put off dealing with sin? What would we do if today was our last chance to make things right?

4. Read Joel 2:12–13. What were the signs in Israel's culture to show they were repentant? How do people demonstrate true repentance today?

5. How does a life of confession change as we become more spiritually mature?

6. What is involved in the process of letting go of sin? Write out a plan for dealing with a specific sin.

Points to Ponder

"God wants us to know the depth of our sins—and let our hearts break over them—so that we can truly grasp the depth of his love for us in seeking to redeem and restore us." In the *Everyday Matters Bible for Women*, Caryn Rivadeneira talks about having a full understanding of sin and how our whole selves are involved.

- How does sin affect our bodies, minds, and souls? How does God bring restoration to each part?

In Psalm 103:12, we find a joyous David proclaiming, "He has removed our sins as far from us as the east is from the west." God reminds us that we have assurance of forgiveness from him, but sometimes it's ourselves we can't forgive.

- How can hanging onto sin be a false comfort or form of control? How does abandoning our sin leave us open to God's unlimited love and call on our life?

So now we can rejoice in our wonderful new relationship with God because our Lord Jesus Christ made us friends of God. (Romans 5:11)

Prayer

God, you know me and you help me to know myself. Help me to be found in you. So much in my life pulls me away from making you the one thing I seek. Thank you for not only showing me the path but giving me your strength and peace.

Add your prayer in your own words.

Amen.

Put It into Practice

This week, identify sin that needs to be confessed. Work with a trusted mentor or friend to take an honest look at any blind spots. Work toward restoration.

Take-away Treasure

It's hard to look at ourselves honestly. When we look at our lives honestly, we see the truth—the truth of pain from the damage our sin has caused, the truth of God's love, greater than any obstacle that would try to get in the way. This is where confession happens and where God calls us to follow him in newness of life, to abide and not hide, to hold out the hurt for him to heal.

CHAPTER 3

Bad Patterns

Breaking the Cycle of Brokenness

For you are my hiding place;
you protect me from trouble.
You surround me with songs of victory.

PSALM 32:7

For this study, read Psalm 32 and Hebrews 5:1–10 and 6:5–14.

The bright running shoes are laced up, the earbuds are in, the door is wide open, and we're ready to go. The music is an important part of the run, selected to boost our energy and our spirits. Nobody listens to a dirge when they start a running routine, so why do we play a soundtrack of negativity in our heads—dwelling on our weaknesses—as we set out on the race of the life of faith? Or perhaps we don't set out on the race out all, instead suppressing our failures until they come out in depression. We try to lift the haze, but the clouds reappear and we're not sure why. We are back on the merry-go-round of regrets. What is the soundtrack in your head? Is it a victory song or is it the woe-is-me on repeat?

What are we waiting for? God calls us to joy. At first glance it might not seem obvious, but a life of confession is a life of joy, of living honestly with ourselves and the world. "Yes," David reminds us, "what joy for those whose record the Lord has cleared of guilt, whose lives are lived in complete honesty!" (Psalm 32:2). The alternative is gut-wrenching guilt, apathy, and doubt. This is the listless misery David describes: "When I refused to confess my sin, my body wasted away, and I groaned all day long" (Psalm 32:3). We have been there, and we too have to do something with it. We can ignore it, sulk, or sigh—or just say the words our hearts long to hear: "I am sorry." Here is a litany that leads to joy. God longs for us to lay it all at his feet—come, abide, dwell, be made whole.

God wants us to be overcomers. But we know that there are sins that seem to keep us stumbling instead of climbing, instead of running. How do we break free, out of the habit of sin? How do we start a new habit of a healthy heart? We come again before God and we're sure he's tired of hearing about this same problem. The woman at the well had been living a bad pattern, but as Jesus pieced together the broken pieces he found what she was truly looking for. Why are we doing what we are doing? Do we really want love? Do we really want joy? We've been going about it all wrong. We need to identify the bad patterns and look for the better path.

God gives us the answer to how we can be overcomers. "So Christ has truly set us free. Now make sure that you stay free" (Galatians 5:1). Paul urges you to "use your freedom to serve one another in love" (Galatians 5:13), to "let the Holy Spirit guide your lives" (Galatians 5:16). A life in the Spirit produces "love, joy, peace, patience, kindness,

goodness, faithfulness, gentleness, and self-control"
(Galatians 5:22–23).

What do we surround ourselves with? Do we surround
ourselves with godly examples, with people who will build
us up? Confession helps to shine a spotlight onto our lives.
God brings his light, but he doesn't want us to just keep it
for ourselves. He wants us to share it with others. When
we practice the root discipline of confession, we are able to
branch out and let the other spiritual disciplines blossom in
our lives. We live in the fruit of the Spirit instead of return-
ing to the rotten apple of repeated sin. When we draw near
to God in confession, he draws near to us: "I will guide you
along the best pathway for your life. I will advise you and
watch over you" (Psalm 32:8).

When we come closer to God we can bring others with us.
Our struggle with sin is not ours alone. We can partner with
others in facing things we can't face alone. God has given
us each other to hold each other accountable, to help each
other out. When we keep silent, we not only hold on to sin
but we don't let the painful lessons help anyone else. We
share our stories not as a way to compare or judge, but as a
way to work together to build up each other in faith. When
we humble ourselves, we lift up Christ and we are able to
lift up others as well.

When the woman at the well encountered Jesus, her excitement overflowed: "The woman left her water jar beside the
well and ran back to the village, telling everyone, 'Come
and see a man who told me everything I ever did! Could
he be the Messiah?'" (John 4:28–29). Because of her, many
believed. She had the victory song. She was ready for a new
start, ready to begin again.

"Father in Heaven! Hold not our sins up against us but hold us up against our sins so that the thought of You when it wakens in our soul, and each time it wakens, should not remind us of what we have committed but of what You did forgive, not of how we went astray but of how You did save us!" —*Søren Kierkegaard*

As you study this chapter, think about what might be holding you back from running the race.

1. What are we afraid of when it comes to confession? How does God overcome those fears?

2. Isaiah 43:1–2 offers words of comfort and forgiveness. How well does God know us? What do we need to discover about ourselves?

3. How does confessing to others help us examine the deeper consequences of sin? Is it easier to tell God or others about our sin? Why? Write down one person you need to confess to, and try to find an appropriate way to make amends.

4. How does confession help us engage our faith? How has sin kept us on the sidelines of something God was calling us to do?

5. Do we see anyone who is making the same mistakes we made whom we could help or pray for?

6. Honesty is the best policy, but how honest do we need to be? Should we tell everything?

Points to Ponder

Hebrews 3:7 talks about the distance we place between ourselves and the truth: "Today when you hear his voice, don't harden your hearts."

- How have you turned the volume down on the voice of God in your life? Is there an area where you have hardened your heart?

In her *Everyday Matters Bible for Women* reflection Anne Jackson says that "when we bring our sin into the light, God's glory shines. It shows a hurting world that there's grace and hope beyond brokenness."

- What part do we play in breaking the pattern of another's brokenness and sin? What is the difference between reveling in and revealing another's sin? How can we partner with others in breaking the pattern of sin?

"People are curious to know the lives of others, but slow to correct their own. Why are they anxious to hear from me what I am, when they are unwilling to hear from thee what they are?" —St. Augustine of Hippo, Confessions

Prayer

God, your purity demands perfection. I strive but I still sin. Yet in that place where all seems lost, you save me by your loving grace. Help me to turn away from well-packaged false promises. Remind me of the victory I have in you. Dwell in me so that I might dwell in your peace.

Add your prayer in your own words.

Amen.

Put It into Practice

This week, find ways to surround yourself with markers of victory. Replace the daily soundtrack of negativity with reminders of the fruits of the Spirit. As Joni Eareckson Tada writes in her article, "Taking 'Little' Sins Seriously," in the *Everyday Matters Bible for Women*: "If you're tired of your struggle against sin, if you're weary of its subtle deceit or the way it hardens your heart, don't give up. Instead, be ready and willing to confess, turn to God, and strive to be holy. Invite God to give you a sensitive conscience and a fresh love for the things that please and delight him."

Take-away Treasure

Confession helps us claim our victory in Christ. We are brought back to truth, and we awake not just to the reality of sin but to the power that God has given us over it. Our discipline is daily dwelling in the promises of God instead of dwelling on our problems.

CHAPTER 4

Hearts That Heal

Spreading Renewal

Share each other's burdens, and in
this way obey the law of Christ.

GALATIANS 6:2

For this study, read Psalm 25 and Galatians 6:1–10.

There is this space at the beginning of our Sunday worship
service where we pause. It may be the longest pause I take
all week. We stop to reflect and examine ourselves; we stop
to confess. "Most merciful God, we confess to you that we
have sinned against you in thought, word, and deed. . . ." I
look at the floor. I close my eyes for half a second and try
to think of something not so bad. For a brief moment, in
my head I review the video of my deed, but my mind hits
Stop. I don't want to see it any further because I know how
it plays out. I blurt out a quick prayer for forgiveness and
the service moves on. But I am reminded how little I pause
for reflection. Do I let the confession I have spoken sink in?
What is the distance between thought and deed? Is there
space there for God?

The confession continues, ". . . by what we have done and by what we have left undone." That's the part that gets me: What is left undone. Just when I thought maybe I could get off the hook, I am humbled. "Remember, it is sin to know what you ought to do and then not do it" (James 4:17). In that one little word of *omission*, I am back to where I started. Søren Kierkegaard talks about focusing on the good and getting out of the way so the good can emerge. Could confession really help us to look at the good and not just the bad? Could confession be a brainstorming session of the good? What is the good left undone in my family, in my neighborhood, in my community, in my city, in my country, in my world?

In *Purity of Hearts Is to Will One Thing*, Kierkegaard searches out that necessary space for self-reflection:

> The press of busyness into which one steadily enters further and further, and the noise in which the truth continually slips more and more into oblivion, and the mass of connections, stimuli, and hindrances, these make it ever more impossible for one to win any deeper knowledge of himself. It is true that a mirror has the quality of enabling a man to see his image in it, but for this he must stand still. If he rushes hastily by, then he sees nothing.

We need to find time in our lives to pause, to create space for empathy. In that quick second, so much can happen—so many words we wish we could take back, so much wrenching pain. It was only a moment, but in the pause we see eternity. Together our scars and burdens have become his own. In his strength we are able to carry others, to care and to comfort. As we confess we are able to bless others through the Spirit working in us. There is more at stake than our own happiness when we come together to confess. In this space we find others, we find the cause and the cost, the pain and the punishment. We find the broken down. When we look around, we see not just our sin but the sin of the whole world.

Paul gives us the antidote to our smug self-righteousness: "Instead, use your freedom to serve one another in love" (Galatians 5:13), and "If you think you are too important to help someone, you are fooling yourself. You are not that important" (Galatians 6:3). When we put God and others first we see our real worth. What is important is the restoration of lives and relationships. What matters more—people or tasks? Do our tasks facilitate our relationships? Are our lives centered on people? What matters more, and how do we show it with our time and actions? How do we live out the law of love? Our task is to "gently and humbly help" (Galatians 6:1), to restore the person to the right road, acknowledging that we have been there too. We confess to others and in the process we help them and not just ourselves. Our lives are not our own.

In community, we confess, and as we share the Peace of Christ, we spread renewal. We are made new in Christ—laying at the cross the things we have done and left undone. In communion, God welcomes us. We receive his body that was broken for us so that we could be restored and made whole, and the work of spreading this renewal can begin. A life of confession plays a part in the restoration of others as well as ourselves. At the end of the worship service, we can truly give thanks and appreciate the blessing that goes with us—the blessing poured out each day as we live in humility and hope: "Go in peace to love and serve the Lord."

*Lead me by your truth and teach me, for
you are the God who saves me. All day long
I put my hope in you. (Psalm 25:5)*

**As you study this chapter, think of the small
steps you can take to spread renewal.**

1. Confession is the beginning of healing, but God calls us to go further. We don't want to deal with the causes or consequences of our sin, but this is where God can give us greater healing. Read Numbers 5:7 and discuss this example of how to make things right.

2. What part do we play in the sin of others? How does our silence affect them? What do we need to speak up and speak out about?

3. How does forgiveness play a role in restoration?

4. In Daniel 9:1–19, Daniel prays for the collective sins of the people. How does he respond when sin is revealed? What are the collective sins that God is calling us to repent of as a society and how should we respond?

5. Make a list of organizations and groups that help bring restoration and renewal to lives. Look for ways to support and offer your help. How can your group get involved?

6. Sometimes people just need a listening ear and a safe space to lay down their burdens. How can you cultivate a community that hears and accepts others whose pain has overtaken their lives? How can sharing your own testimony be a powerful way to help others?

Points to Ponder

In Galatians 6:1, Paul writes: "If another believer is overcome by some sin, you who are godly should gently and humbly help that person back onto the right path."

- Are we allowing sins that we ourselves do not commit?

- How can we confront the sin of others and help restore their relationship with God?

"God cannot give us a happiness and peace apart from Himself, because it is not there."
—C. S. Lewis, Mere Christianity

Prayer

God, when I look back, I see all the cracks along the path that I have caused through my sin. But you didn't let me fall through and you helped fix the broken places. Thank you for your forgiveness. Continue your healing work and help me to share the joy you have given. When others fall short, help me to come alongside them with your love. When I realize I have been silent toward injustice, help me find my voice. Give us the tools to use for the renewal of all things.

Add your prayer in your own words.

Amen.

Put It into Practice

This week, think of an area in your life where God has brought healing and wholeness and find five things you can do to help others in that same situation. Write them down, set some goals, and share them with someone who can keep you accountable.

Take-away Treasure

The healing work that started in us is not just for us. God brings wholeness and restoration in us so that through us his life-giving love can be shared. Confession is just the start. In big and small ways, we can help bring others back to God's forgiveness and mercy.

Notes / Prayer Requests

Notes / Prayer Requests

_____

_____

_____

_____

_____

_____

_____

_____

_____

_____

_____

_____

_____

_____

_____

_____

_____

_____

Leader's Guide to Prayer & Confession

Prayer

It takes a lot of time and dedication to be a leader, but be encouraged as you study—your prayers and example will help others to pray and continue the chain of impact and blessing. As the leader, you set the tone. Take the time to share your own prayer journey and come as a learner and listener. Prayer takes us to a place of vulnerability. Find ways to incorporate the discipline of prayer seamlessly into your time together. Seize moments for spontaneous prayer. We grow in study not just by talking about the practice of prayer, but also by putting it into practice as the Spirit leads.

Thoughts on Praying Together

- Not everyone is comfortable praying aloud in a group setting. Vary your practice throughout your meeting. You can select prayers in the Bible or by others that can be spoken or read silently. Create settings for praying in small groups or one on one. Everyone's voice and perspective can offer valuable insight.

- Let songs and worship be part of your prayer time together. Incorporate creative ways to pray through movement, journaling, and art. Encourage participants to gather examples and share how they see prayer in different ways.

Prayer Prompts

Brainstorm on prayer prompts as a group and try a different one between meetings. Here are some ideas:

- Take a prayer walk through your community.

- Have group members look for favorite prayers.

- Start a prayer chain.

- Assign each day on your calendar a different concern or person/group to pray for.

- Pray through the news.

- Spend time in nature, letting God speak through creation.

Incorporating Other Disciplines

- *Invite silence.* Incorporate a time of silence into your times together. Ask participants to identify both places and times where they find silence during their daily routine.

- *Welcome simplicity.* Encourage group members to replace one distraction in their life with prayer.

- *Embrace solitude.* Find space for solitude. You could even assign one meeting time as a time for solitude and have group members report back at the next meeting.

- *Remember rest.* We don't have to be *on* all the time. Evaluate your times of physical, emotional, and spiritual rest. Are there lots of time fillers that aren't really nourishing? Encourage members to take a day of Sabbath rest and also to find daily Sabbath moments. Invite them to share their experiences.

- *Join worship.* Our prayers take on many forms, and the focus of our joy is praising God. Incorporate music and songs into your time together. Have a scavenger hunt for worship throughout your week. Have group members bring back songs and moments of worship they encountered.

Additional Resources

- *Praying the Jesus Prayer Together* by Brother Ramon and Simon Barrington-Ward

- *Exploring Prayer* by Sue Mayfield

- *The Practice of the Presence of God* by Brother Lawrence

- *The Everyday Matters Journal*

- Go to prayernotebookapp.com, an organizational tool for prayer recommended by Ann Voskamp

- Go to instapray.com, which helps you connect with others around the world in prayer

One Last Thing

The commitment that you have made to pray with and for each other doesn't have to end with this study. Look for ways to continue your practice of prayer and see the impact—whether through prayer partners or a designated time to pray as a group, even if you can't still meet together. You will be encouraged and reminded that you are not alone in the journey.

Confession

We start with the truth, so get ready to go deep. We all live with the fallout of our failings, but we are not here to beat ourselves up about it. Instead, we are learning to overcome and grow together. The ultimate truth of our vibrant life of faith in Christ gives us the joy we can keep coming back to. There will be bumps along the way, but together we are becoming stronger. You will be helping to build bonds and shape habits that will last beyond your times of study and reflection. Encouragement and patience will come in handy, so take some time for yourself first to walk your way through the study. Find points from your own life that might resonate with your group. Something beautiful is about to emerge!

Setting Some Ground Rules

Create a safe space for discussion. Talk to a pastor or professional counselor about being available and encourage participants to meet with them if they feel the need.

- Cultivate care and understanding. Your attitude and actions will help set the tone. Your own sharing will help others. Establish a rapport of trust and confidentiality.

- Begin and end with hope and joy. Always bookend your times together with the knowledge of our assurance in Christ that we are forgiven and free (John 15:9–11).

- Think of ways to encourage the group in between your meetings. Set up times for prayer. Draw names or have prayer partners to encourage one another.

Thoughts on Ways to Incorporate the Psalms

- The Psalms include such vital examples of confession, which is why a psalm has been included with each chapter.

- Encourage participants to read the psalm between meetings for their own time of study and reflection.

- Have participants reflect on the Psalms and write their own psalm as a way to practice confession.

- In between your meetings, have participants look for other psalms that have powerful examples of confession.

Incorporating Other Practices

- *Grant forgiveness.* Steep yourselves in God's forgiveness through his word. Have group members look for areas in their lives where they are holding on to bitterness and resentment. Ask the tough questions of what holding on to that is doing to their lives and what forgiveness would look like.

- *Cultivate gratitude.* Spend time together focused on thankfulness. Share specific things you are thankful for about each other and about the ways God is working in your lives.

- *Seek justice.* We are tasked with working toward justice in our own lives and on behalf of others. Help group members identify those who need justice, and think of ways you can be an advocate on their behalf.

- *Work toward reconciliation.* Identify individual and communal areas where reconciliation is needed. Brainstorm how your group or faith community can be involved. Often this is not a one-time act but an ongoing process. What can be put in place to sustain this work?

- *Appreciate silence.* Incorporate an intentional extended time of silence in your times together. Consider going on a reflection-focused retreat as a group or individually.

Follow Up

Stay in touch with your fellow study participants and see how you can encourage each other along your journey. Look for opportunities for fellowship, find different ways to connect and communicate—even a simple note. Don't underestimate what your words can do and the power they have to build up others.

Additional Resources

- *Confessions* by St. Augustine

- *Slaying your Giants* by Kent Crockett

- *Forgiveness and Reconciliation: Spiritual Practices for Everyday Life*

- *The Everyday Matters Journal*

One Last Thing

We have done some tough work through our time together, but the growth doesn't stop here. Look for ways to continue the good work. Connect participants with a spiritual advisor or mentor. Create a group project. How can God turn our sorrows into joy and create something beautiful? How can our confessions help others? Use your creative resources to make a visual or musical testimony of God's faithfulness. Volunteer as a group with an organization that works toward mercy, restoration, and healing.

EVERYDAY MATTERS BIBLE STUDIES
for women

Spiritual practices for everyday life

Acceptance	Mentoring
Bible Study & Meditation	Outreach
Celebration	Prayer
Community	Reconciliation
Confession	Sabbath & Rest
Contemplation	Service
Faith	Silence
Fasting	Simplicity
Forgiveness	Solitude
Gratitude	Stewardship
Hospitality	Submission
Justice	Worship